# Jam Session

## *John Elway*

**Denis Dougherty**
**ABDO Publishing Company**

## visit us at
## www.abdopub.com

Published by ABDO Publishing Company, 4940 Viking Drive, Suite 622, Edina, Minnesota 55435. Copyright © 1999 by Abdo Consulting Group, Inc. International copyrights reserved in all countries. No part of this book may be reproduced in any form without written permission from the publisher.

Printed in the United States.

Cover and Interior Photo credits: AP/Wide World Photos

Edited by Terri Dougherty

Sources: Knight-Ridder News; New York Times; People Magazine; Sports Illustrated; Sports Illustrated For Kids; The Sporting News; USA Today

### Library of Congress Cataloging-in-Publication Data

Dougherty, Denis.
    John Elway / Denis Dougherty.
       p. cm. -- (Jam Session)
Includes index.
Summary: Examines the personal life and football career of the quarterback for the Denver Broncos.
ISBN 1-57765-040-9 (hardcover)
ISBN 1-57765-342-4 (paperback)
1. Elway, John, 1960-   --Juvenile literature.   2. Football players--United States--Biography--Juvenile literature.   3. Denver Broncos (Football team)--Juvenile literature.
   [1.Elway, John, 1960-   .  2. Football players.]   I. Title. II. Series.
GV939.E48D68   1999
796.332'092--dc21
   [B]
                                                                                  98-19167
                                                                                      CIP
                                                                                       AC

# Contents

*Super Day for a Superstar* ............................................. *4*
*First Down Denver!* ...................................................... *6*
*A Star is Born, and Raised* ........................................... *8*
*High School Heroics* .................................................... *11*
*Two Sport Standout* ..................................................... *12*
*Denver's Gift of Hope* .................................................. *14*
*The Drive to Stardom* .................................................. *16*
*The Ring is the Thing* .................................................. *18*
*Rocky Mountain Low* ................................................... *20*
*California, Here We Come* ........................................... *22*
*No. 7 in Seventh Heaven* ............................................. *24*
*Elway's Stats* ............................................................... *26*
*Chronology* .................................................................. *28*
*Glossary* ...................................................................... *30*
*Index* ............................................................................ *32*

# Super Day for a Superstar

**Q**uarterback John Elway stood calmly in the pocket as the NFL's battle zone raged around him.

The score was 17-17 late in the third quarter of Super Bowl XXXII in San Diego. John's Denver Broncos, at the Green Bay Packers' 12-yard line, faced third down and needed six yards for a first down.

The Broncos' veteran leader looked for an open receiver. All were covered. Meanwhile, the Packers' huge defensive linemen were breaking through John's protective offensive line. What's a 37-year-old quarterback to do?

An ordinary quarterback would take a sack, or throw the ball away and let kicker Jason

John Elway holds the Vince Lombardi Trophy after winning Super Bowl XXXII.

Elam give Denver a 20-17 lead. But John has never been an ordinary quarterback.

John tucked the football under his arm and ran. He met Packers all-pro safety LeRoy Butler near the first-down marker. Butler ducked his head to crush John.

But John leaped into the air, and was spun around by Butler's hit. He took another shot from safety Mike Prior. Somehow, he made it to the Green Bay four-yard line. Thanks to John's guts and determination, Terrell Davis scored moments later to give the Broncos a 24-17 lead.

John Elway prepares to hand off the ball to Broncos running back Terrell Davis.

# First Down Denver!

**L**ike most teams, Green Bay feared John for his cannon-like throwing arm. But on January 25, 1998, John hurt the Packers most with his legs and his great will to win.

John ran for two first downs in the Super Bowl and also scored Denver's second touchdown. In the end Denver won 31-24, giving John the first Super Bowl victory of his brilliant 15-year career.

"This guy is almost 40 years old, and he is laying his life and body on the line," Broncos linebacker John Mobley said after the game. "So I told the defensive guys that we needed to have the same intensity to get this thing done."

John had quarterbacked the Broncos in three previous Super Bowls, all losses. But that became ancient history. After the game, the victorious quarterback stood before an army of microphones, cameras, and lights.

"I was afraid to imagine this," John told reporters. "I didn't want to imagine it, but

**Elway scampers in for a touchdown during Super Bowl XXXII.**

it's three times better than anything I could have imagined."

Fans everywhere were happy for him. Even the beaten Packers paid their respects to the conquering hero.

Packers quarterback Brett Favre said: "He's had a great career and he finally got the greatest thing the NFL has to offer. I'm really happy for him."

John Elway had been an amazing athlete his whole life. He could throw bullet passes for touchdowns. He frustrated defensive linemen with his quickness and uncanny knack for avoiding tacklers. He pulled victories from the clutches of defeat. He even played professional baseball.

But this was his greatest moment. He was finally a champion.

John Elway celebrates a Bronco Super Bowl victory.

# A Star is Born, and Raised

Sports have been part of John Albert Elway's family for generations. His grandfather, Harry Elway, quarterbacked a semipro Pennsylvania team. His mother, Jan, was a high school athlete. His father, Jack, played quarterback in high school, and coached high school and college football.

"From the time John was a boy he's been at football practice," Jack Elway said. "Watching. Absorbing. Now he amazes me with what he knows about football."

John's father had a busy schedule. But he made time to throw the baseball to John, play basketball in the driveway with him, and toss the football around with his son.

"I was always the first to quit in whatever we played," Jack Elway said. "As he grew older, I thought, 'Is he as good as I think he is?'"

When John was eight, he won his hometown Punt, Pass, and Kick competition. "I learned to be competitive, to try to get better every time out," John said. "I learned to be a good winner and a good loser. But I also learned never to be satisfied with losing. That just made me try harder next time."

John has a twin sister, Jana, and an older sister, Lee Ann, who also love competition. Jack raised his children to put leadership and hard work above personal glory and statistics.

John continued to work hard as he got older. He was often the first one in the Broncos' meeting room and set records in the team's weight room.

"Any time you can look out and see a guy that's a part of your team as determined as he is to win, it's contagious," former Broncos linebacker Simon Fletcher said. "Elway has proven that good things happen if you never give up."

John's family moved often, following his dad's coaching career. When John's father got a job coaching at California State University in Northridge, Jack scouted area high school coaches to see who could teach his son the most. That's how the family decided to live in the Los Angeles suburb of Granada Hills.

John Elway (left) with mother Jan and father Jack Elway.

Elway playing in the East-West Shrine Game at Stanford Stadium in 1983.

# High School Heroics

John had a stellar high school career at Granada Hills. By the time he was a senior, he was the most highly recruited high school football player in the United States.

As a junior John passed for more than 3,000 yards. During his senior year, he completed 129 of 200 passes for 1,837 yards and 19 touchdowns. A knee injury in the sixth game ended his high school football career.

John had knee surgery and recovered fully. He was named to the *Parade*, *Scholastic Coach*, *Football News*, and National Coaches Association All-America teams. John had a sparkling 3.8 grade point average as well.

John also loved to play baseball. During his senior year he led Granada Hills to the Los Angeles City Baseball Championship. He had a .491 batting average, a 4-2 pitching record, and was named Los Angeles city high school Player of the Year.

He was so good the Kansas City Royals chose him in the 1979 summer draft. But John decided to go to college at Stanford instead.

# Two Sport Standout

John was a two-time All-America quarterback at Stanford. He set five NCAA Division I-A records and nine major Pac-10 Conference records. He finished second in the Heisman Trophy balloting his senior year.

**Elway playing for Stanford University.**

Former San Francisco 49ers and Stanford coach Bill Walsh called John, "probably the best college quarterback I've ever seen."

John was also a standout outfielder on the Stanford baseball team. As a freshman he batted .269 with one home run. He hit .349 with nine homers as a sophomore, his final college baseball season.

"I love to take two steps into a fly ball and then hum it home, just let it fly and watch it move," John said of baseball. "There's no feeling like that."

During the summer of 1982, after his junior year in college, John played for the

New York Yankees' Class A team in Oneonta, N.Y. He hit .318 and threw out nine base runners in 42 games.

His ability in baseball and football gave him good bargaining leverage when it came time for him to negotiate a football contract.

John Elway announced April 26, 1983 that he would play baseball for the New York Yankees rather than sign with the Baltimore Colts as the top draft choice of the NFL.

# Denver's Gift of Hope

The 1983 NFL draft was the year of the quarterback, with John heading the list of talented signal callers. John was chosen by the Baltimore Colts with the first pick of the draft. But John's style didn't mesh with Colts owner Robert Irsay and coach Frank Cush.

John decided if he wasn't traded that he would continue playing professional baseball for the New York Yankees. The Colts decided to trade him to Denver. When Broncos fans learned the talented quarterback was heading their way, Elwaymania took hold. Reporters crowded training camp. A local newspaper started an Elway Watch. "Elway is life for us," one Bronco fan said.

John strutted into Denver with his wobbly gait, flashed his huge smile, and captured the hearts of Broncos fans.

"You only find a quarterback like John once in a lifetime," Broncos owner Pat Bowlen said years later. "John Elway's value to the Denver Broncos, to this city, to the state of Colorado isn't something you can really measure."

**Elway stands in the pocket looking for a receiver.**

Denver fans expected a lot of their new star, and it took John a while to adjust to his role. His receivers had to learn to catch passes so powerful they could shred gloves and bruise chests, and John wasn't used to coach Dan Reeves' complicated offense.

Reeves benched John and started veteran quarterback Steve DeBerg midway through the season. But when DeBerg was injured late in the season, John got another chance. He composed himself, showing great running and throwing ability.

"I hate to fail," John said a few seasons later. "My rookie year was the first time I'd ever been faced with something where nothing came easy."

Denver finished 9-7 and made the playoffs for the first time since 1979. In his first playoff appearance, John threw for 123 yards, completing 10 of 15 passes, and rushed for 16 yards. The Broncos lost to Seattle, 31-7, but Elway gave the team and the city hope.

John started 14 of 16 games the next season. The Broncos went 13-3, the team's most wins ever to that point, and won the division.

**The Broncos franchise is in John Elway's hands.**

# The Drive to Stardom

John is considered the best quarterback ever at bringing a team back from the brink of defeat. His most memorable feat is known as "The Drive," a remarkable performance against Cleveland in the 1986 AFC Championship Game.

The game was played in Cleveland in front of almost 80,000 screaming fans. With under six minutes left in the game, the Broncos were behind 20-13. Denver was on its own two-yard line.

Things looked bleak, but John was confident as he moved the team down the field. With under two minutes remaining on the

John Elway (7) eludes the Cleveland Browns in what was known as "The Drive."

clock, it was third-and-18. Was a first down possible? Yes! John hit Mark Jackson with a 20-yard pass to keep the drive alive.

From the five-yard line with 39 seconds left, he again passed to Jackson. Touchdown! John had moved the team 98 yards in 15 plays to tie the game 20-20.

In overtime, John calmly moved the team 60 yards down the field. Rich Karlis kicked a 33-yard field goal. The Broncos were on their way to the Super Bowl!

"There is no question John can be the greatest two-minute quarterback ever," Reeves said. "He's got that arm."

**John Elway prepares to send the ball downfield en route to a 23-20 overtime victory in the 1986 AFC Championship game against the Cleveland Browns.**

# The Ring is the Thing

Denver lost to the New York Giants in Super Bowl XXI, and fell to Washington the next season in Super Bowl XXII. John was the NFL's MVP in 1987, but the team didn't have enough talent to win it all. Denver again won the AFC title in 1989. But the Broncos lost to San Francisco 55-10 in Super Bowl XXIV, the worst defeat in Super Bowl history. John, however, kept his focus on winning the ring.

"I have a vision of getting a perfect team and winning a Super Bowl ring even if it means getting beat 10 times," John said after the third Super Bowl loss. "I just want another chance to win it."

John's dream didn't come true right away. Denver lost the 1991 AFC Championship Game to Buffalo and stumbled under Reeves. Some thought John was getting too old to take the pounding delivered in an NFL game, but Pat Bowlen defended him.

"There's a perception that Superman can't fly anymore. That's nonsense. We wouldn't trade John Elway for any quarterback in football," Bowlen said.

By 1995, John had nine surgeries on his shoulders, elbow, foot, and knee. But he didn't question his physical condition. "I've always had a bad walk," he said. "I know I don't have the quickness I once did, but I'm still learning, still getting better. I honestly don't feel like I'm done yet."

John's former quarterback coach and offensive coordinator Mike Shanahan arrived as head coach in 1995. The two friends teamed up to rebuild the Broncos.

"John Elway has been the right quarterback for any kind of offense," Shanahan said. "We could draw plays in the sand and he'll find a way to get it done."

John thrived under Shanahan, and was determined to win a Super Bowl ring.

"That's really the one thing I have left to accomplish," John said. "We've won AFC championships. We've won big games. We've had great comebacks. The statistics are nice, but I want to win the ring."

John Elway is sandwiched by New York Giants Leonard Marshall (70) and Jim Burt (64) during one of his Super Bowl losses.

# Rocky Mountain Low

In 1996 it looked like Denver was unstoppable. John was at the top of his game in leading Denver to 12 wins in its first 13 games. "I always thought (Miami's) Dan Marino was the perfect quarterback," John said. "But I think I'm something else. I think I'm a football player."

In the ninth game of the season, against Oakland on Monday Night Football, John worked his comeback magic once again. With a little more than four minutes left, Oakland led 21-16. In just 47 seconds, John turned the game around. He drove the team 73 yards for a touchdown and a Broncos victory.

"When you play John, the clock has to read 0:00 before you can be sure of a victory," Raiders receiver Tim Brown said.

But late in the season John's leg hurt, and he missed a loss at Green Bay. The team dropped two of its final three games and couldn't get its momentum back. Denver faced Jacksonville in an AFC playoff game. In one of the NFL's biggest upsets ever, the Jaguars, who had only been in the league two seasons, beat the Broncos 30-27 in Denver.

"I can't imagine how John must feel," Brett Favre said. "To keep being disappointed like he has been, it's got to be horrible."

John was crushed. For a month he spoke to few people. "I've been deep, deep undercover just because I don't want to rehash it," he said. "I'm not sure if I'll ever get over it. That's as disappointed as I've ever been. You can talk about Super Bowl (losses) or anything. There's not one that comes close to that one."

He even considered retiring. "It's too early now to make a decision because I think it would be a snap decision, so I wanted to take some time," he said after the loss. "For this season, I'd say I'm probably (going to play), but it's not definite. I'm going to take a long time and keep rehashing to see where I am."

**John Elway is dejected after the heavily favored Broncos fell to the Jaguars.**

# California, Here We Come

The next season, John was back. But it looked like his career might be over when he injured his throwing arm in a preseason game against Miami. "I was scared," he said of the injury. "After it happened I thought, 'Maybe I'm done.'"

But he recovered quickly and was there when the 1997 regular season opened. The Broncos jumped out to a 9-1 record. However, Denver suffered road losses at Kansas City, Pittsburgh, and San Francisco. Denver entered the playoffs as a wild-card team. The 1980 Oakland Raiders were the only wild-card team ever to win the Super Bowl. Denver had

*John Elway (7) runs past Pittsburgh Steelers linebacker Jason Gildon (92) while leading the Broncos to an AFC Championship and a trip to California.*

a rematch with Jacksonville in its first playoff game. The Broncos got their revenge with a 42-17 win. In the next game at Kansas City, John once again directed a game-winning, fourth-quarter touchdown drive as Denver won 14-10.

In the AFC title game at Pittsburgh, John threw two touchdown passes in the second quarter as Denver grabbed a 24-14 halftime lead. But Pittsburgh scored late in the fourth quarter to cut the deficit to 24-21.

With 61,382 fans screaming at them, the Broncos faced a third-and-six on their own 15 with two minutes left. If Denver did not get a first down, Pittsburgh would get the ball back with a chance to win.

John called the play: All Pivot. "John," tight end Shannon Sharpe yelled, "we don't have that play."

"We do now," John shot back. "Just go get open."

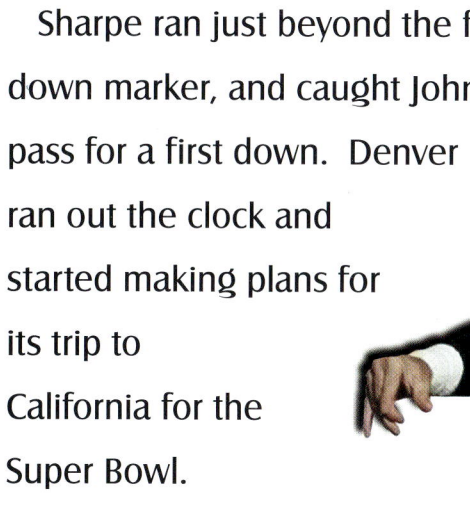

John Elway fires a pass and leads the Broncos over the Jaguars in the playoffs.

Sharpe ran just beyond the first-down marker, and caught John's pass for a first down. Denver ran out the clock and started making plans for its trip to California for the Super Bowl.

## No. 7 in Seventh Heaven

The Broncos were huge underdogs as they prepared to meet the Packers in Super Bowl XXXII. But John wasn't shaken. "As soon as (the Pittsburgh game) was over I started thinking about the game," John said. "Satisfied? I'm not satisfied yet. We've won AFCs before. If we can win one more, I'll be satisfied."

John knew he might lose the game. He prepared his four children for that possibility and told Jessica, Jordan, Juliana, and Jack he still loved them no matter what happened in the Super Bowl.

"All you have to do is win once, and it can erase a lot of bad memories," John said just before the Super Bowl.

Late in Super Bowl XXXII, the Broncos got the ball on the Packers' 49-yard line. The score was 24-24.

There was 3:27 left. John had the Packers right where he wanted them. No quarterback in NFL history has been better than John at pulling out dramatic fourth-quarter victories.

Denver Broncos quarterback John Elway scrambles during the third quarter of Super Bowl XXXII.

Sure enough, No. 7 marched Denver to the winning touchdown. Mixing Terrell Davis' runs with a 23-yard pass to fullback Howard Griffith, John finally scaled the NFL's highest mountain. The Broncos beat the Packers in one of the most exciting Super Bowls ever.

"There have been a lot of things that have gone along with losing three Super Bowls and playing for 14 years and kind of being labeled a guy who's never been on a winning Super Bowl team," John said. "It makes this that much sweeter."

In 15 seasons, John led his team to 138 victories, more than any NFL quarterback ever. He is the fourth-leading rushing quarterback in NFL history. He went over the 3,000-yard passing mark 12 times, tying Dan Marino for the NFL record.

John will certainly be in the Pro Football Hall of Fame some day. John once said, "My goal is to be the best quarterback ever." Most people believe he has accomplished his goal.

**John Elway celebrates after a Bronco touchdown during Super Bowl XXXII.**

# Elway's Stats

## Profile

Born: June 28, 1960

Home: Englewood, Colorado

Height: 6 feet, 3 inches

Weight: 215 pounds

High School: Granada Hills (California)

College: Stanford (California)

Pros: Selected as the first pick of the 1983 NFL draft by the Baltimore Colts. Traded to Denver on May 2, 1983.

Personal: Married to Janet, a swimmer at Stanford he met during his freshman year in college. They have four children: Jessica, Jordan, Juliana, and Jack. John works with The Elway Foundation and owns and operates seven car franchises in the Denver area.

## Honors

Named to Pro Bowl (1986, 1987, 1993, 1994, 1996, 1997)

NFL MVP (1987)

AFC Player of the Week (14 times)

AFC Offensive Player of the Month (October 1996, November 1997)

## Records

Most fourth-quarter game-winning drives (41)

Most regular-season wins by an NFL starting quarterback (138)

Most 3,000-yard passing seasons (12, tied with Dan Marino)

Only player to pass for more than 3,000 yards and rush for more than 200 yards in seven straight seasons (1985-1991). Also accomplished this feat in 1994, 1996, and 1997.

Most rushing attempts by a quarterback.

Only John and former Minnesota Vikings quarterback Fran Tarkenton have passed for 40,000 yards and rushed for 3,000 yards in their careers.

# Chronology

**June 28, 1960** - John Elway was born in Port Angeles, Washington.

**1979** - Led the Granada Hills High School baseball team to the Los Angeles city championship. Had a .491 batting average and a 4-2 pitching record.

- Was the most highly recruited high school athlete in the nation.
- Made the following All-America teams: *Parade, Scholastic Coach, Football News* and National Coaches Association.
- Was selected by the Kansas City Royals in the summer baseball draft.
- Signed letter of intent to attend college at Stanford in the Northern California city of Palo Alto.

**1981** - Played final season of college baseball, batting .349 with nine homers and 50 runs batted in.

- Was the first selection of the New York Yankees in the summer baseball draft.

**1982** - Played baseball for the New York Yankees' Class A farm club in Oneonta, New York. Had .318 average and 24 RBI.

- Ended college football career with five major NCAA Division 1-A records and nine major Pac-10 records.
- Named consensus All-American.
- Finished second in Heisman Trophy balloting.

**1983** - Earned degree in economics from Stanford.

- First player selected in the NFL draft. Chosen by the Baltimore Colts and traded to the Denver Broncos.
- Started 10 games for the Broncos. Team ended his rookie season with a 9-7 record and a loss in the first round of the playoffs.

**1984** - Started 14 games, completing 214 of 380 passes for 2,598 yards. Also rushed for 237 yards, third highest on the team.

**1985** - Set Broncos single-season records for pass attempts (605), completions (237), passing yards (3,891), rushing and passing plays (656), and total offense (4,414).

**1986 season** - Completed "The Drive" in the final minutes against Cleveland in January, 1987, to lift Broncos to their first AFC championship since 1977.

- Completed 22 of 37 passes for 304 yards in Super Bowl XXI. Broncos lose to the New York Giants, 39-20.
- Named to the Pro Bowl.
- Honorable mention on the All-NFL team.
- All-AFC second team.

**1987 season** - Named NFL's Most Valuable Player.
- Led team to AFC Championship Game victory over Cleveland, throwing for three touchdowns and 281 yards.
- In Super Bowl XXII, completed 14 of 38 passes for 257 yards, ran for 32 yards and became first quarterback in Super Bowl history to catch a pass. Broncos lose to the Washington Redskins, 42-10.
- Starting quarterback in the Pro Bowl.
- Named to All-NFL and All-AFC teams.
- Named AFC MVP.

**1989 season** - In AFC Divisional Playoff Game against Pittsburgh, moved the Broncos 80 yards late in the fourth quarter to and threw the winning touchdown in a 24-23 victory.
- Led Broncos to AFC Championship Game win over Cleveland, throwing for 385 yards and three touchdowns and gaining 25 of his 39 rushing yards on one play.
- In Super Bowl XXIV, completed 10 of 26 passes for 108 yards. Scored Denver's only touchdown on a three-yard run. Broncos lose to the San Francisco 49ers, 55-10, the worst loss in Super Bowl history.

**1991 season** - In AFC Divisional Playoff Game against Houston, rallied Broncos from 21-6 deficit to 26-24 victory.

**1992** - Named NFL Man of the Year for his work with the non-profit Elway Foundation.

**1993 season** - AFC MVP.
- AFC Offensive Player of the Year.
- AFC Player of the Year.
- Named to the UPI All-AFC team and AP's second-team All-NFL.
- Starting quarterback in the Pro Bowl.

**1994 season** - Named to the Pro Bowl.

**1996 season** - Starting quarterback in the Pro Bowl.
- Second team All-Pro.
- First team All-AFC.
- Second in NFL MVP voting.
- AFC MVP.
- Set NFL record for all-time victories by a starting quarterback.

**1997 season** - Threw career-high 27 touchdown passes.
- Selected as Pro Bowl starter.
- Led Broncos to their first Super Bowl victory, 31-24 over the Green Bay Packers in Super Bowl XXXII.

# Glossary

**CENTER** - The player in the middle of the offensive line who snaps the football between his legs to the quarterback to start a play.

**DEFENSIVE LINE** - Several players who line up opposite the offensive line and try to tackle the player with the ball.

**DRAFT** - The National Football League's method of allowing teams to choose players from college teams.

**FIRST DOWN** - The first of four chances the offense has to gain 10 yards or cross the goal line.

**GUARD** - Player on the offensive line who lines up between the tackle and center.

**HEISMAN TROPHY** - Awarded each year to the best college football player in America.

**LINEBACKER** - A player on defense who lines up behind the defensive line. Typically makes tackles on running plays, defends against short passes or rushes the passer.

**MVP** - Most Valuable Player. The MVP Award is given to the top player in the NFL each season.

**OFFENSIVE LINE** - Several players who line up opposite the defensive line and protect the quarterback on passing plays or block for running backs on running plays.

**PLAYOFFS** - Postseason games played by division winners and wild-card teams.

**POCKET** - Area protected by the offensive line from which the quarterback tries to pass.

**QUARTERBACK** - Player on offense who calls the signals for the plays. He gets the ball from the center and usually runs, passes, or hands the ball to a running back.

**SACK** - To tackle the quarterback behind the line of scrimmage.

**SUPER BOWL** - The National Football League's championship game, played by the champion of the American Football Conference (AFC) and the champion of the National Football Conference (NFC).

**TAILBACK** - Offensive player who lines up farthest behind the line of scrimmage. He is the running back who gets the ball on most running plays.

**WILD-CARD** - A playoff team that did not win its division but has a good enough record to qualify for the postseason.

# Index

## A
AFC Championship Game 16, 18, 29
AFC playoff game 20
AFC title 18, 23
All-America team 11, 28

## B
Baltimore Colts 14, 26, 28
Bowlen, Pat 14, 18
Brown, Tim 20
Butler, LeRoy 5

## C
California State University 9
college football 8, 28

## D
Davis, Terrell 5, 25
DeBerg, Steve 15
Denver Broncos 4, 14, 28

## E
Elway, Harry 8

## F
family 8, 9
Favre, Brett 7, 20
*Football News* 11, 28
football practice 8

## G
Granada Hills 9, 11, 26, 28
Green Bay Packers 4, 29
Griffith, Howard 25

## H
Heisman Trophy 12, 28
high school 8, 9, 11, 26, 28

## J
Jackson, Mark 17

## K
Kansas City Royals 11, 28

## M
Marino, Dan 20, 25, 27
Mobley, John 6
Monday Night Football 20
MVP 18, 26, 29

## N
NCAA 12, 28
New York Giants 18, 28
New York Yankees 13, 14, 28
NFL draft 14, 26, 28
NFL history 24, 25

## O
Oakland Raiders 22
offense 15, 19, 28

## P
Pennsylvania 8
Player of the Year 11, 29
playoffs 15, 22, 28
Pro Football Hall of Fame 25
professional baseball 7, 14

## R
Reeves, Dan 15
rookie 15, 28

## S
San Diego 4
San Francisco 49ers 12, 29
Shanahan, Mike 19
Sharpe, Shannon 23
Stanford 11, 12, 26, 28
summer draft 11
Super Bowl 6, 17, 18, 19, 21, 22, 23, 24, 25, 28, 29

## T
"The Drive" 16, 28
touchdowns 7, 11, 29

## W
Walsh, Bill 12